Oh! My SPEAKING 1

CEDU BOOK

UNIT COMPONENTS

• KEY PATTERNS

Key words and key patterns are presented in context.
Students can role-play the conversation used in the cartoon.

• VOCABULARY

Vocabulary words can be used immediately through activities related to pattern sentences.

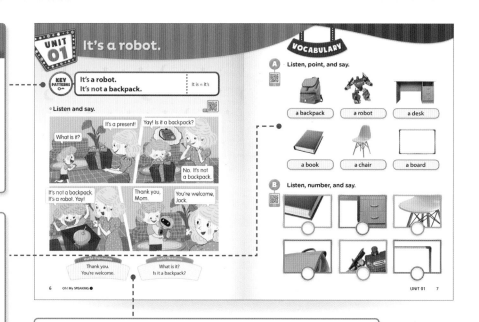

• USEFUL EXPRESSIONS & QUESTIONS

A variety of particularly useful expressions from the dialogues in the cartoons allow students to develop their speaking skills.

• KEY PATTERN PRACTICE

Repeating sentences with key patterns helps students to naturally remember what they have learned.

• LISTEN AND SPEAK

Substituting words in key patterns in a combined listening and speaking activity assists students to build their speaking fluency.

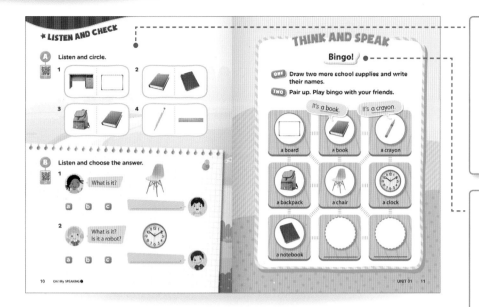

LISTEN AND CHECK

★ LISTEN AND CHECK

A Listen and circle.

1   2

3   4

B Listen and choose the answer.

1 What is it?
   ⓐ   ⓑ   ⓒ

2 What is it?
   Is it a robot?
   ⓐ   ⓑ   ⓒ

THINK AND SPEAK

Bingo!

ONE Draw two more school supplies and write their names.

TWO Pair up. Play bingo with your friends.

It's a book.   It's a crayon.

a board   a book   a crayon

a backpack   a chair   a clock

a notebook

• LISTEN AND CHECK

Listening practice gets students to relate the key sentences to the pictures and to learn how to use the right sentences in the conversation.

• THINK AND SPEAK

A fun and educational communication game gets students to practice key sentences repeatedly.

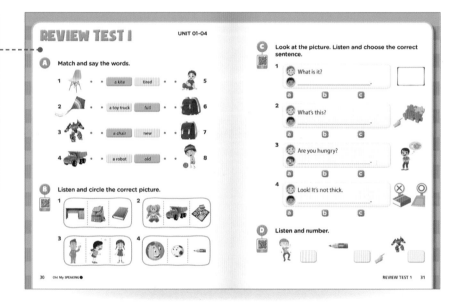

REVIEW TEST

Word reviews and a variety of speaking and listening activities help students recall and further practice key words and key patterns from previous units.

REVIEW TEST 1

UNIT 01-04

A Match and say the words.

1   a kite   tired   5
2   a toy truck   full   6
3   a chair   new   7
4   a robot   old   8

B Listen and circle the correct picture.

1   2

3   4

C Look at the picture. Listen and choose the correct sentence.

1 What is it?
   ⓐ   ⓑ   ⓒ

2 What's this?
   ⓐ   ⓑ   ⓒ

3 Are you hungry?
   ⓐ   ⓑ   ⓒ

4 Look! It's not thick.
   ⓐ   ⓑ   ⓒ

D Listen and number.

UNIT 01 It's a robot.

A Unscramble the words.

1   2

3   4

B Look and write.

1   It's a

2   It's not a

C Trace and write.

a crayon   a ruler   a chair   a clock   a desk

1   What is it?
    It's

2   Is it a crayon?
    No, It's not.
    It's

3   What is it?
    It's

4   Is it a clock?
    Yes, It's

...choose the right answer for the blank.

What is it?   Yay! Is it a backpack?
No
...not a backpack   Thank you, Mom   You're welcome, Jack.

ⓐ It's a robot   ⓑ It's a present
ⓒ It's not a backpack

Choose one item and complete the sentence.

It's

WORKBOOK

Various writing, listening, and speaking exercises allow students to review key words and key patterns learned in the Student Book.

CONTENTS

UNIT 01

It's a robot.

KEY PATTERNS

It's **a robot.**
It's **not a backpack.**

It is = It's

● **Listen and say.**

What is it?

It's a present!

Yay! Is it a backpack?

No. It's not a backpack.

It's not a backpack.
It's a robot. Yay!

Thank you, Mom.

You're welcome, Jack.

Useful Expressions

Thank you.
You're welcome.

Useful Questions

What is it?
Is it a backpack?

A Listen, point, and say.

a backpack

a robot

a desk

a book

a chair

a board

B Listen, number, and say.

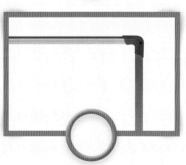

★ KEY PATTERN PRACTICE

A Listen and say.

| What is it? | Is it a backpack? |

It's a backpack.

Yes. It's a backpack.

No. It's not a backpack.

a backpack   a robot   a desk   a book   a chair   a board

B Pair up. Then practice.

What is it?

It's _____.

Is it a robot?

No. It's not a robot. It's _____.

⭐ LISTEN AND SPEAK

A Listen, point, and say.

05

What is it?

It's _____.

Is it _____?

Yes. It's _____.

No. It's not _____.

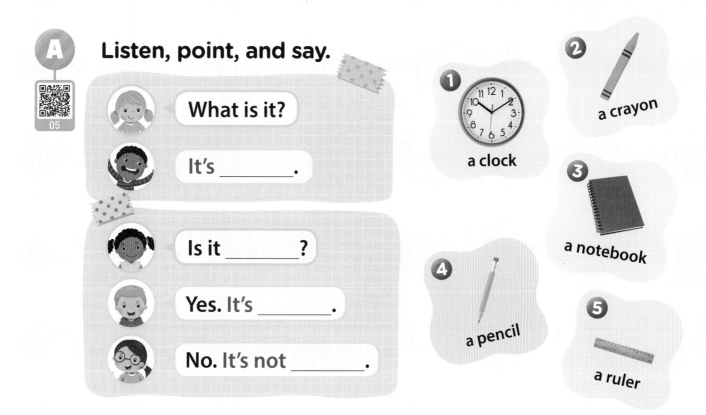

1 a clock

2 a crayon

3 a notebook

4 a pencil

5 a ruler

B Listen and say.

06

1 What is it?

It's _____.

2 Is it a book?

No. It's not _____.
It's _____.

YOUR TURN! Talk about the things in your room.

What is it?

★ LISTEN AND CHECK

 A Listen and circle.

1

2

3

4

 B Listen and choose the answer.

1 What is it?

 a   b   c

2 What is it?
Is it a robot?

 a   b   c

THINK AND SPEAK

Bingo!

ONE Draw two more school supplies and write their names.

TWO Pair up. Play bingo with your friends.

It's <u>a book</u>.

It's <u>a crayon</u>.

a board

a book

a crayon

a backpack

a chair

a clock

a notebook

This is a toy truck.

KEY PATTERNS

This is a toy truck.
That's a toy car.

That's
= That is

Listen and say.

09

Nice to meet you. I'm Jack.

Nice to meet you, too. I'm Wacky.

What's this?

This is a toy truck.

What's that?

That's a toy car.

This is my toy truck, and that's your toy car.

Wow! This is my toy car. Thank you.

Useful Expression

Nice to meet you.

Useful Questions

What's this?
What's that?

A Listen, point, and say.

a toy truck

a doll

a ball

a puzzle

a toy car

a kite

B Look, match, and say.

1

a kite

2

a toy truck

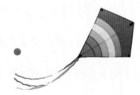

3

a doll

★ KEY PATTERN PRACTICE

A **Listen and say.**

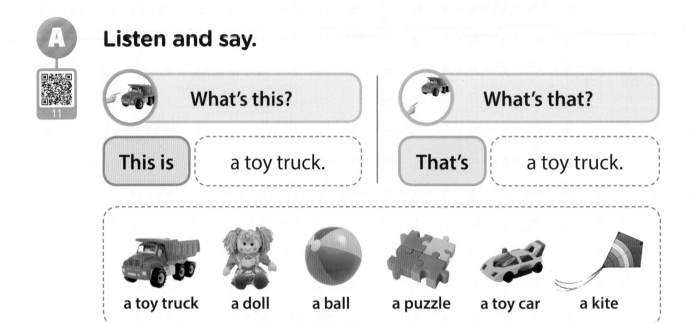

B **Pair up. Then practice.**

★ LISTEN AND SPEAK

A Listen, point, and say.

What's this?

This is _____.

What's that?

That's _____.

4 a teddy bear

5 a jump rope

6 a yo-yo

3 a top

1 a computer game

a board game 2

B Listen and say.

1

What's that?
That's _____.

2

What's this?
This is _____.

3

What's that?
That's _____.

YOUR TURN! Introduce your toys to your friends.

What's this?

★ LISTEN AND CHECK

A Listen and choose the answer.

1
ⓐ   ⓑ

2
ⓐ   ⓑ

3
ⓐ   ⓑ

B Listen and number.

THINK AND SPEAK

Find the matching cards.

ONE Put all the cards face up on the table.

TWO Memorize the position of each card within 10 seconds.

THREE Turn all the cards face down and find the matching cards. Upon finding the matching card, say either "This is _____." or "That's _____."

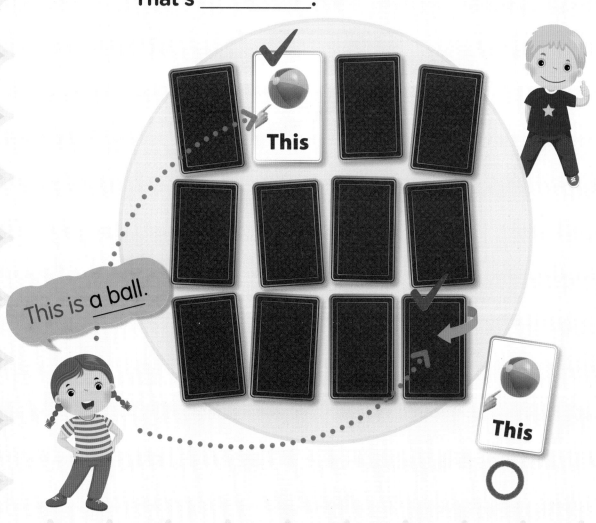

This

This is a ball.

This

I'm hungry.

KEY PATTERNS

I'm hungry.
I'm not tired.

I'm = I am

Listen and say.

I'm hungry.
Are you hungry, too?

Yes. I'm hungry, too.
Let's go home.

I'm full.
Thank you, Mom.

You're welcome.

Are you okay, Wacky?

No. I'm not okay.
I'm tired.

Now, are you still tired?

No. I'm not tired.
I'm okay! Thank you.

Useful Expression

Let's go home.

Useful Questions

Are you hungry, (too)?
Are you still tired?

A Listen, point, and say.

| hungry | full | tired |
| okay | angry | sad |

B Follow and say.

1 2 3 4

hungry   sad   angry   okay

★ KEY PATTERN PRACTICE

A Listen and say.

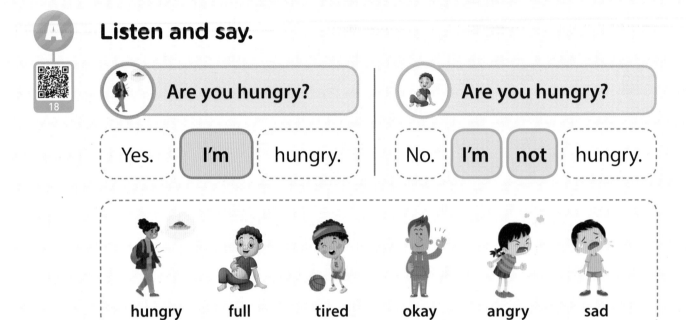

Are you hungry?

Yes. | **I'm** | hungry.

Are you hungry?

No. | **I'm** | **not** | hungry.

hungry   full   tired   okay   angry   sad

B Pair up. Then practice.

Are you _____?

Yes. I'm _____.

Are you tired?

No. I'm not tired. I'm _____.

⭐ LISTEN AND SPEAK

A Listen, point, and say.

😊	Are you _____?
🧒	Yes. I'm _____.
👧	No. I'm not _____.

1 thirsty

2 sick

3 sleepy

4 scared

5 bored

6 excited

B Listen and say.

1
Are you sleepy?
Yes. I'm_____.

2
Are you bored?
No. I'm not_____.
I'm_____.

3
Are you scared?
Yes. I'm_____.

 YOUR TURN! Ask about your friends' feelings.

Are you happy?

★ LISTEN AND CHECK

A Listen and check.

1

2

3

4

B Listen and choose the answer.

1

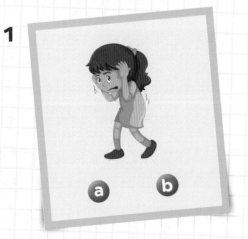

2

THINK AND SPEAK

Mime the feeling.

ONE Choose one of the vocabulary flashcards. Mime the feeling to your friend.

TWO Have your friend guess what it is. Mime until your friend gets it right. Then switch.

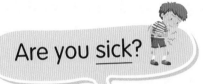

Are you sick?

No. I'm not sick.

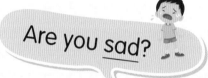

Are you sad?

No. I'm not sad.

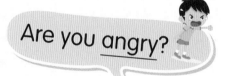

Are you angry?

Yes. I'm angry.

UNIT 04

It's a big monster.

KEY PATTERNS

It's (not) **big.**
It's (not) **a big monster.**

It's = It is

Listen and say.

Useful Expression

I see.

Useful Question

Is it a short pencil?

Listen, point, and say.

big
a big ball

small
a small ball

old
an old backpack

new
a new backpack

short
a short pencil

long
a long pencil

B

Listen and match.

1 big •   • backpack •

a long pencil

2 new •   • pencil •

a big ball

3 long •   • ball •

a new backpack

★ KEY PATTERN PRACTICE

A   Listen and say.

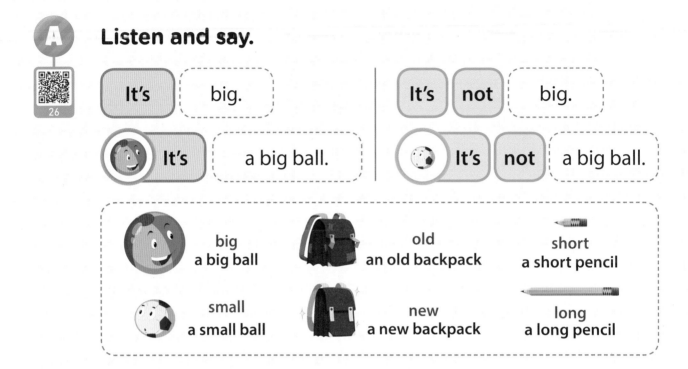

It's   big.   It's | not | big.

It's   a big ball.   It's | not | a big ball.

big
a big ball

old
an old backpack

short
a short pencil

small
a small ball

new
a new backpack

long
a long pencil

B   Pair up. Then practice.

It's not ___small___ .

It's not ___ _____ _____ .

It's ___ _____ _____ .

It's ___long___ .

It's _a_ _long_ _pencil_ .

★ LISTEN AND SPEAK

A Listen, point, and say.

It's _____.
It's __ __ __ _____.

It's not _____.
It's not __ __ __ _____.

1 clean
a clean doll

2 dirty
a dirty doll

3 soft
a soft teddy bear

4 hard
a hard board

5 thin
a thin book

6 thick
a thick book

B Listen, check, and say.

1
It's not _____.
It's _____.

2
It's _____.
It's __ _____
_____ _____.

3
It's not _____.
It's _____.

YOUR TURN! Describe your school objects and toys.

It's a short pencil.

★ LISTEN AND CHECK

A Listen and circle.

1
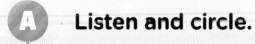

2

3

4
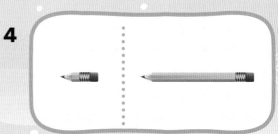

B Listen and number.

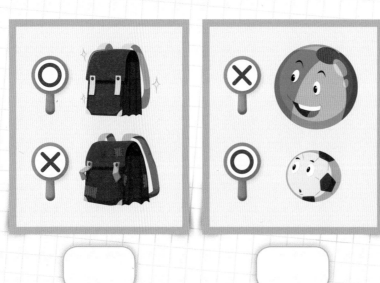

THINK AND SPEAK

Describe the thing together.

ONE Pair up.

TWO Choose and describe any school object or toy.

THREE Take turns to describe it as below.

It's a ball.

It's new.

It's a new ball.

REVIEW TEST I

A Match and say the words.

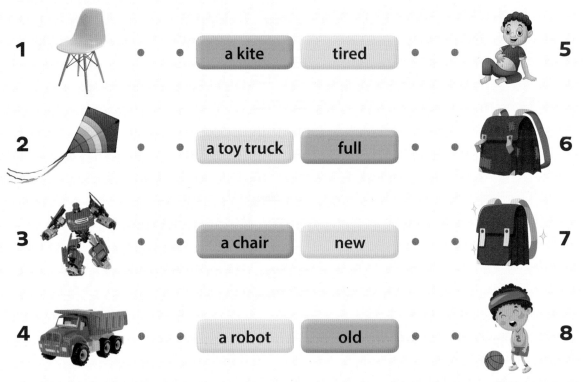

1 • • a kite | tired • • 5

2 • • a toy truck | full • • 6

3 • • a chair | new • • 7

4 • • a robot | old • • 8

B Listen and circle the correct picture.

C Look at the picture. Listen and choose the correct sentence.

1

😊 What is it?

🙂 _____.

a   b   c

2

😊 What's this?

🙂 _____.

a   b   c

3

😊 Are you hungry?

😟 _____.

a   b   c

4

😊 Look! It's not thick.

🙂 _____.

a   b   c

D Listen and number.

E **Introduce your toy.**

STEP 1 Choose and write the correct words for each blank.

It's new   a new robot   This is a robot

This is my toy.

Is this a toy truck?

No. This is not a toy truck.
_____.

Is it new?

Yes. _____.
It's _____.
This is my friend.

Wow!

STEP 2 Draw your toy.

STEP 3 Write about your toy.
Introduce your toy to your friends.

This is my toy.

This is a _____.

It's _____.

I love my toy!

He's my dad.

KEY PATTERNS

He's/She's my **dad/grandma.**
He's/She's **smart.**

He's = He is
She's = She is

Listen and say.

Who's he?

He's my dad.
He's smart.

Who's she?

She's my grandma.
She's kind.

Who's she?

She's my sister.
She's shy.

Who's he?

How small!

This is my baby brother.

Useful Expression

How small!

Useful Questions

Who's he?
Who's she?

VOCABULARY

Listen, point, and say.

35

dad   mom   grandma   brother   sister

smart   kind   shy   active

B

Listen and match.

36

1    2    3   4

★ KEY PATTERN PRACTICE

A Listen and say.

Who's he?			Who's she?		
He's	**my**	dad.	**She's**	**my**	mom.
He's		smart.	**She's**		kind.

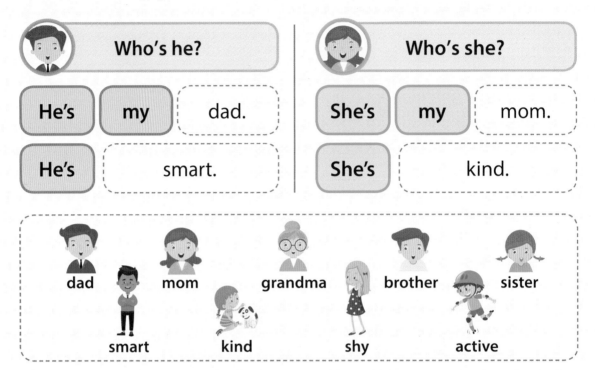

dad   mom   grandma   brother   sister

smart   kind   shy   active

B Pair up. Then practice.

Who's he?

Who's she?

He's my _____.
He's _____.

She's my _____.
She's _____.

1 dad

2 brother

3 grandma

4 sister

★ LISTEN AND SPEAK

A Listen, point, and say.

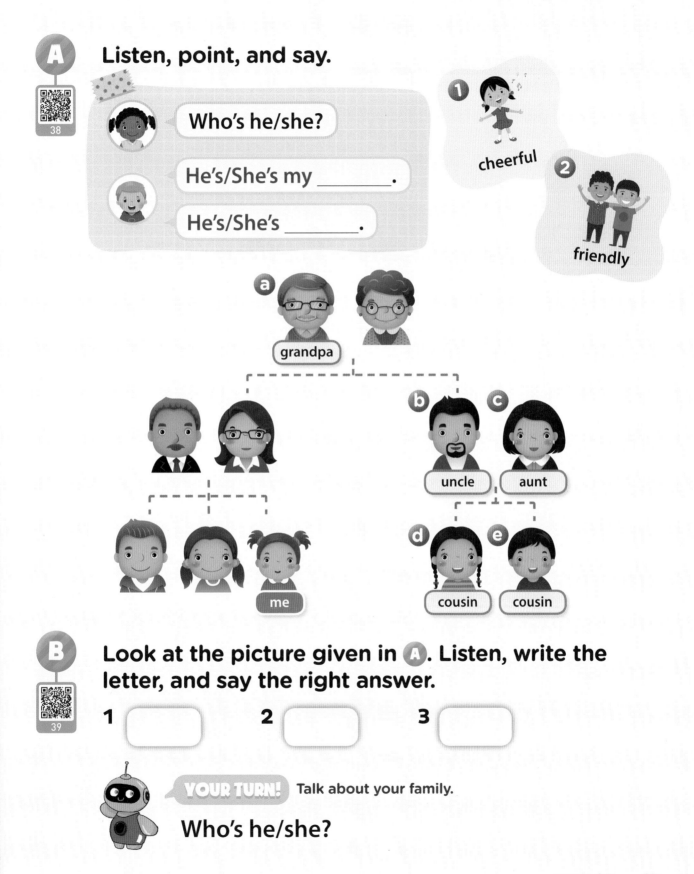

Who's he/she?

He's/She's my _____.

He's/She's _____.

1 cheerful

2 friendly

a grandpa

b uncle c aunt

me

d cousin e cousin

B Look at the picture given in **A**. Listen, write the letter, and say the right answer.

1 [ ] 2 [ ] 3 [ ]

YOUR TURN! Talk about your family.

Who's he/she?

A Listen and check.

1

2

3

4

B Listen and choose the answer.

1

Who's he?

a   b   c

2

Who's she?

a   b   c

THINK AND SPEAK

Show and Tell - Family Tree

ONE Draw your family and talk about them with a friend.

Who's she?

She's my <u>mom</u>.
She's <u>kind</u>.

Who's he?

He's my <u>brother</u>.
He's <u>smart</u>.

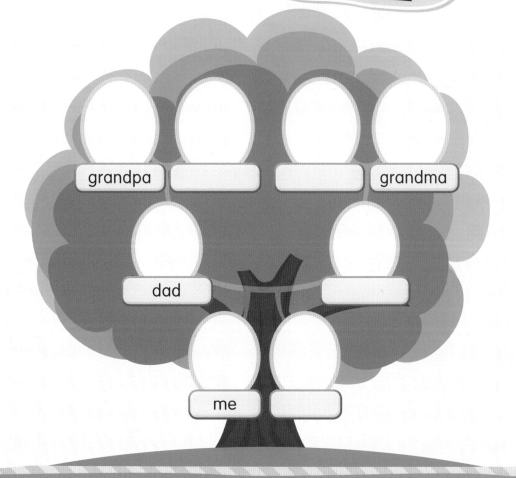

grandpa

grandma

dad

me

UNIT 06

Is it tall?

Is it tall?
It's (not) tall.

It's = It is

Listen and say.

Look! A giraffe!

Is it tall?

Yes. It's tall.

Wow! A bear!

Is it big?

Yes! It's big and strong.

Watch out! Is it a snake?

Eek! It's a snake. It's long.

Is it a rock?

No. It's a turtle. It's slow.

Useful Expression

Watch out!

Useful Question

Is it a snake?

VOCABULARY

A Listen, point, and say.

| tall | fast | slow | strong | weak |

| a bear | a turtle | a snake | a giraffe |

B Look, match, and say.

1  **2**  **3**  **4**

| weak | fast | strong | slow |

★ KEY PATTERN PRACTICE

A **Listen and say.**

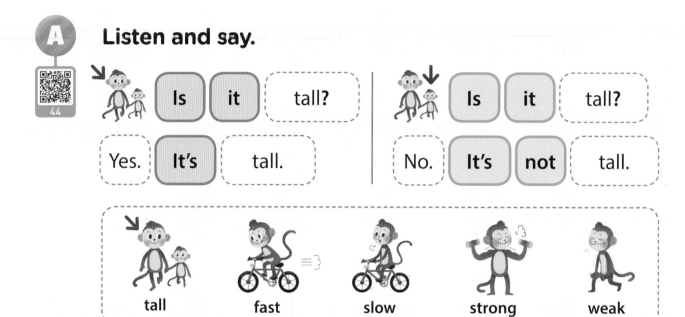

Is it tall?

Yes. It's tall.

Is it tall?

No. It's not tall.

tall fast slow strong weak

B **Pair up. Then practice.**

1 strong

2 slow

3 long

4 tall

Is it _strong_?

Yes. It's _strong_.

Is it _____?

No. It's not _____.
It's _____.

✦ LISTEN AND SPEAK

Listen, point, and say.

> Is it _____?

> Yes. It's _____.

> No. It's not _____.

1 heavy

2 light

3 noisy

4 quiet

5 tiny

B

Listen and say.

1

Is it tiny?

Yes. It's _____.

2

Is it heavy?

No. It's not _____.
It's _____.

3

Is it noisy?

Yes. It's _____.

YOUR TURN! Describe animals.

Look! Is it tall?

★ LISTEN AND CHECK

Listen and check.

1

2

3

4

B Listen and choose the answer.

1

2

THINK AND SPEAK

Describe the animal.

ONE Draw one animal in the center and write as many adjectives as you can.
Add more arrows if you need to.

TWO Show and tell with your friends.

tall	short	fast	slow	strong	weak
heavy	light	noisy	quiet	tiny

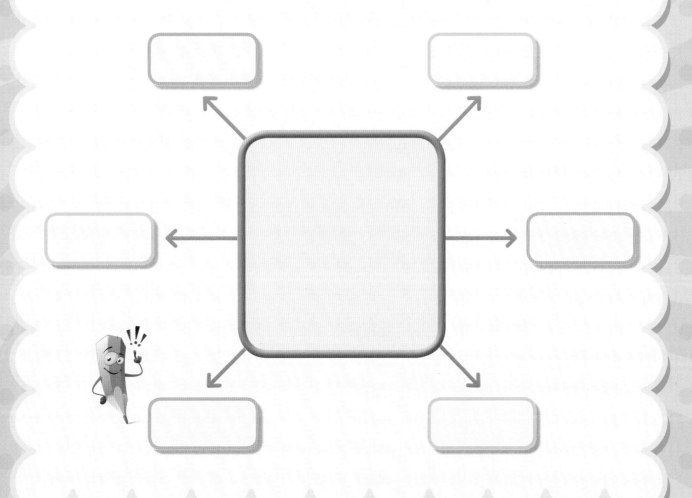

They're dogs.

They're dogs.
They're not rabbits.

They're =
They are

Listen and say.

Useful Expressions
Look at them.
They're good friends.

Useful Question
Are they dogs?

VOCABULARY

A Listen, point, and say.

dogs

turtles

rabbits

cats

hamsters

parrots

B Follow and say.

1

2

3

4

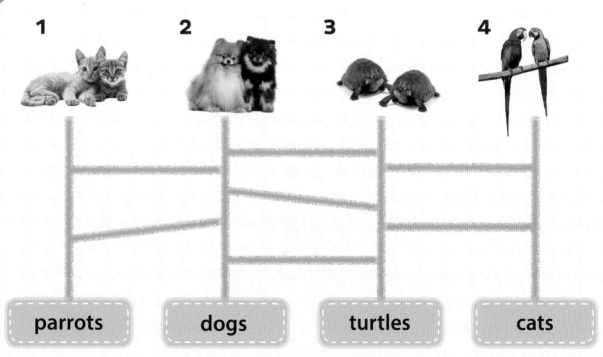

parrots

dogs

turtles

cats

★ KEY PATTERN PRACTICE

A Listen and say.

Are they dogs?

| Yes. | **They're** | dogs. |

Are they dogs?

| No. | **They're** | **not** | dogs. |

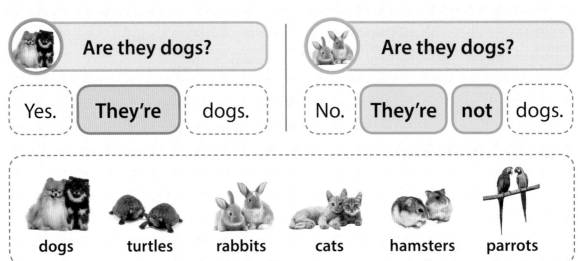

dogs · turtles · rabbits · cats · hamsters · parrots

B Pair up. Then practice.

Are they _____?

Are they dogs?

No. They're not dogs. They're _____.

Yes. They're _____.

✦ LISTEN AND SPEAK

A Listen, point, and say.

Are they _____?

Yes. They're _____.

No. They're not _____.

1 snails
2 chickens
3 pigs
4 beetles
5 frogs

B Listen and say.

1
Are they beetles?
No. They're not ____.
They're _____.

2
Are they pigs?
Yes. They're _____.

3
Are they snails?
Yes. They're _____.

YOUR TURN! Talk about your pets.

Do you have any pets? What are they?

★ LISTEN AND CHECK

A Listen and check.

1

2

3

4

B Listen and choose the answer.

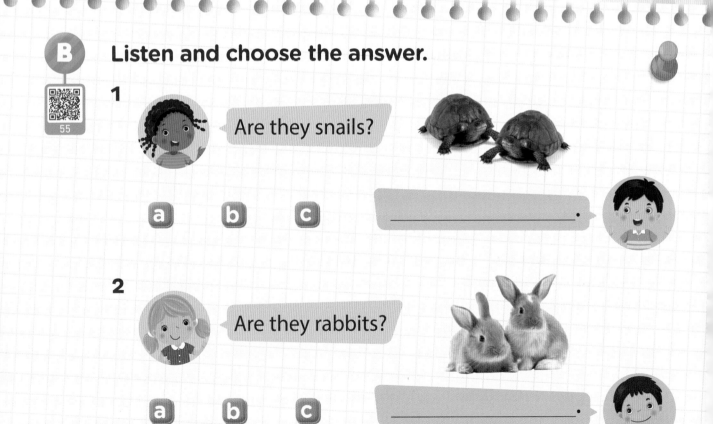

1

Are they snails?

a b c

2

Are they rabbits?

a b c

THINK AND SPEAK

What are they?

ONE Pair up. One person picks up one of the *animal* cards.

TWO Mime and give some hints about the animal until your friend gets it right. Then take turns.

(Picking up one card)
They're <u>slow</u>.
They're not <u>fast</u>.

Are they <u>snails</u>?

No. They're not <u>snails</u>.
(Miming)

Are they <u>turtles</u>?

Yes. They're <u>turtles</u>.

UNIT 08

There's a table.

There's a table.
There are books.

There's =
There is

Listen and say.

Oh no! My phone!

Wacky, what's in the room? Show me.

Let's see. There's a table. There's a sofa.

There are books. There are books on the sofa.

There's your bag.

There it is. There's your phone in the bag.

Useful Expression

There it is.

Useful Question

What's in the room?

A Listen, point, and say.

a table

a sofa

a lamp

a rug

pictures

curtains

B Look, match, and say.

1

2

3

4

a lamp

a sofa

a rug

a table

✦ KEY PATTERN PRACTICE

A Listen and say.

What's in the room?	What's in the room?
There's a table.	**There are** pictures.

 a table   a sofa   a lamp   a rug   pictures   curtains

B Pair up. Then practice.

There's _____.

There are _____.

★ LISTEN AND SPEAK

A   Listen, point, and say.

What's in the room?

There's _____.

There are _____.

① an alarm clock
② a bed
③ mirrors
④ a bookshelf
⑤ a closet

B   What's in the room? Draw and say.

YOUR TURN! Talk about the things in your room.

What's in your room?

★ LISTEN AND CHECK

A Listen and check.

B Listen and number.

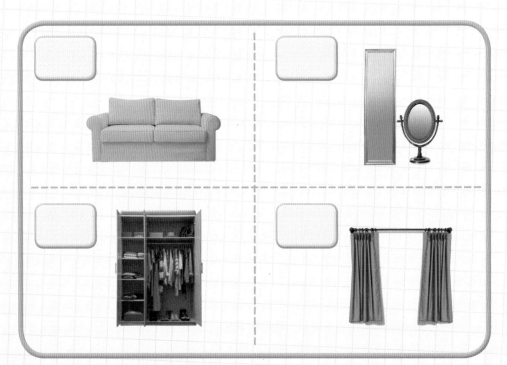

THINK AND SPEAK

Bingo!

ONE Look at and say the words on the board.

TWO Fill in the boxes with your own items.

THREE Pair up. Play bingo with your friend.

There's <u>a bed</u>.

There are <u>curtains</u>.

a bed

curtains

a closet

a lamp

pictures

a table

a sofa

_____

_____

A Match and say the words.

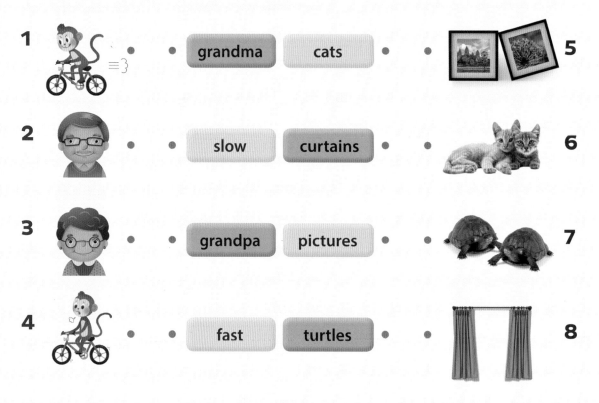

1 • • grandma cats • • 5

2 • • slow curtains • • 6

3 • • grandpa pictures • • 7

4 • • fast turtles • • 8

B Listen and circle the correct picture.

1 2

3 4

C

Look at the picture. Listen and choose the correct sentence.

1

 Who's she?

_____.

a   b   c

2

Is it tall?

_____.

a   b   c

3

Are they rabbits?

_____.

a   b   c

4

What's in the room?

_____.

a   b   c

D

Listen and number.

REVIEW TEST 2

E Introduce your pets.

STEP 1 Choose and write the correct words for each blank.

| They're | Are they | small |

Look at my pets.
They're Jerry and Mary.

What are they?
_____ rabbits?

No. They're not rabbits.
_____ hamsters.

Wow, they're
_____.

They're good friends.
I love my pets.

STEP 2 Draw your pets. If you don't have any, draw a pet you want to have.

STEP 3 Write about your pets.
Introduce your pets to your friends.

Look at my pets. They're _____ and _____.
(name)   (name)

They're _____.
(animal)

They're _____.
(adjective)

I love my _____.
(animal)

SCOPE & SEQUENCE

UNIT 01 It's a robot.

Key Patterns	Vocabulary	Useful Expressions	Goals
It's a robot. It's not a backpack.	a backpack / a robot / a desk / a book / a chair / a board / a clock / a crayon / a notebook / a pencil / a ruler	Thank you. You're welcome. **Useful Questions** What is it? Is it a backpack?	• Asking a question • Identifying objects (school things) • Making affirmative/negative statements ● **Theme** School objects and things in a classroom

UNIT 02 This is a toy truck.

Key Patterns	Vocabulary	Useful Expression	Goals
This is a toy truck. That's a toy car.	a toy truck / a doll / a ball / a puzzle / a toy car / a kite / a computer game / a board game / a top / a teddy bear / a jump rope / a yo-yo	Nice to meet you. **Useful Questions** What's this? What's that?	• Greetings • Introducing objects • Identifying objects (toys) ● **Theme** Toys

UNIT 03 I'm hungry.

Key Patterns	Vocabulary	Useful Expression	Goals
I'm hungry. I'm not tired.	hungry / full / tired / okay / angry / sad / thirsty / sick / sleepy / scared / bored / excited	Let's go home. **Useful Questions** Are you hungry, (too)? Are you still tired?	• Expressing current condition and feelings • Making affirmative/negative statements ● **Theme** Feelings

UNIT 04 It's a big monster.

Key Patterns	Vocabulary	Useful Expression	Goals
It's (not) big. It's (not) a big monster.	big / small / old / new / short / long / clean / dirty / soft / hard / thin / thick / a big ball / a small ball / an old backpack / a new backpack / a short pencil / a long pencil / a clean doll / a dirty doll / a soft teddy bear / a hard board / a thin book / a thick book	I see. **Useful Question** Is it a short pencil?	• Describing • Making affirmative/negative statements ● **Theme** Describing things

REVIEW TEST 1 UNIT 01-04

UNIT 05   He's my dad.

Key Patterns	Vocabulary	Useful Expression	Goals
He's/She's my dad/ grandma. He's/She's smart.	dad / mom / grandma / brother / sister / grandpa / uncle / aunt / cousin / smart / kind / shy / active / cheerful / friendly	How small! **Useful Questions** Who's he? Who's she?	• Introducing family members • Describing characteristics ● **Theme** Family

UNIT 06   Is it tall?

Key Patterns	Vocabulary	Useful Expression	Goals
Is it tall? It's (not) tall.	tall / fast / slow / strong / weak / heavy / light / noisy / quiet / tiny / a bear / a turtle / a snake / a giraffe	Watch out! **Useful Question** Is it a snake?	• Asking information • Describing features ● **Theme** Zoo animals

UNIT 07   They're dogs.

Key Patterns	Vocabulary	Useful Expressions	Goals
They're dogs. They're not rabbits.	dogs / turtles / rabbits / cats / hamsters / parrots / snails / chickens / pigs / beetles / frogs	Look at them. They're good friends **Useful Question** Are they dogs?	• Defining pets • Demonstrative pronoun (Plural) • Making affirmative/negative statements ● **Theme** Pets

UNIT 08   There's a table.

Key Patterns	Vocabulary	Useful Expression	Goals
There's a table. There are books.	a table / a sofa / a lamp / a rug / pictures / curtains / an alarm clock / a bed / mirrors / a bookshelf / a closet	There it is. **Useful Question** What's in the room?	• Identifying objects (furniture and other things) • Making statements • Reporting Singular/Plural ● **Theme** Things in the living room

REVIEW TEST 2   UNIT 05-08

WORD LIST

N

new	25
noisy	43
notebook	9

O

okay	19
old	25

P

parrots	47
pencil	9
pictures	53
pigs	49
puzzle	13

Q

quiet	43

R

rabbits	47
robot	7
rug	53
ruler	9

S

sad	19
scared	21
short	25
shy	35
sick	21
sister	35
sleepy	21
slow	41
small	25
smart	35
snails	49
snake	41
sofa	53
soft	27
strong	41

T

table	53
tall	41
teddy bear	15
thick	27
thin	27
thirsty	21
tiny	43
tired	19
top	15
toy car	13
toy truck	13
turtles	41

U

uncle	37

W

weak	41

Y

yo-yo	15

This

This

This

This

This

This

This is a ball.

That

That

That

That

That

That

That's a puzzle.

UNIT 01

UNIT 01

UNIT 01

UNIT 02

UNIT 01

UNIT 01

UNIT 01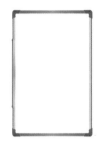

UNIT 02

UNIT 01

UNIT 01

UNIT 01

UNIT 02

UNIT 01

UNIT 01

UNIT 02

UNIT 02

a backpack	a robot	a desk	a book
a chair	a board	a clock	a crayon
a notebook	a pencil	a ruler	a toy truck
a doll	a ball	a puzzle	a toy car

UNIT 02

UNIT 02

UNIT 02

UNIT 03

UNIT 03

UNIT 03

UNIT 02

UNIT 02

UNIT 02

UNIT 03

UNIT 03

UNIT 03

UNIT 03

UNIT 03

UNIT 03

UNIT 03

UNIT 03

UNIT 03

a top	a board game	a computer game	a kite
hungry	a yo-yo	a jump rope	a teddy bear
angry	okay	tired	full
sleepy	sick	thirsty	sad

UNIT 03

UNIT 04

UNIT 04

UNIT 04

UNIT 03

UNIT 04

UNIT 04

UNIT 04

UNIT 03

UNIT 04

UNIT 04

UNIT 04

UNIT 04

UNIT 04

UNIT 04

UNIT 04

scared	bored	excited	big
small	old	new	short
long	clean	dirty	soft
hard	thin	thick	a big ball

VOCABULARY FLASHCARDS

UNIT 04	UNIT 04	UNIT 04	UNIT 05

UNIT 04	UNIT 04	UNIT 05	UNIT 05
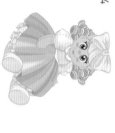			

UNIT 04	UNIT 04	UNIT 04	UNIT 05
	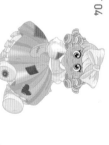		

UNIT 04	UNIT 04	UNIT 05	UNIT 05
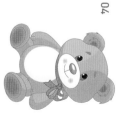	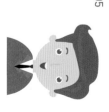		

a small ball	a long pencil	a hard board	mom
an old backpack	a clean doll	a thin book	grandma
a new backpack	a dirty doll	a thick book	brother
a short pencil	a soft teddy bear	dad	sister

UNIT 05

UNIT 05

UNIT 05

UNIT 06

UNIT 05

UNIT 05

UNIT 05

UNIT 06

UNIT 06

UNIT 06

UNIT 05

UNIT 05

UNIT 05

UNIT 06

UNIT 06

UNIT 06

smart	kind	shy	active
grandpa	uncle	aunt	cousin
cheerful	friendly	tall	fast
slow	strong	weak	a bear

UNIT 06

UNIT 06

UNIT 06

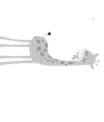

UNIT 06

UNIT 06

UNIT 06

UNIT 06

UNIT 06

UNIT 07

UNIT 07

UNIT 07

UNIT 07

UNIT 07

UNIT 07

UNIT 07

UNIT 07

a turtle	a snake	a giraffe	heavy
light	noisy	quiet	tiny
dogs	turtles	rabbits	cats
hamsters	parrots	snails	chickens

UNIT 07

UNIT 08

UNIT 08

UNIT 07

UNIT 08

UNIT 08

UNIT 08

UNIT 07

UNIT 08

UNIT 08

UNIT 08

UNIT 08

UNIT 08

pigs	beetles	frogs
a sofa	a lamp	a rug
curtains	an alarm clock	a bed
a bookshelf	a closet	

a table	pictures	mirrors

UNIT 01

It's

UNIT 02

This is

UNIT 03

I'm

UNIT 04

It's

UNIT 01

It's not

UNIT 02

That's

UNIT 03

I'm not

UNIT 04

It's not

UNIT 05

He's my

UNIT 05

He's

UNIT 06

Is it

UNIT 06

It's not

UNIT 05

She's my

UNIT 05

She's

UNIT 06

It's

UNIT 07

They're

UNIT 07

They're not

UNIT 08

There are

•

?

UNIT 08

There's

•

•

?

초·등·코·치
천일문 *sentence*

1,001개 통문장 암기로 영어의 기초 완성

1 | 초등학생도 쉽게 따라 할 수 있는 암기 시스템 제시

2 | 암기한 문장에서 자연스럽게 문법 규칙 발견

3 | 영어 동화책에서 뽑은 빈출 패턴으로 흥미와 관심 유도

4 | 미국 현지 초등학생 원어민 성우가 녹음한 생생한 MP3

5 | 세이펜(음성 재생장치)을 활용해 실시간으로 듣고 따라 말하는 효율적인 학습 가능

Role Play 기능을 통해 원어민 친구와 1:1 대화하기!

* 기존 보유하고 계신 세이펜으로도 핀파일 업데이트 후 사용 가능합니다.

* Role Play 기능은 '레인보우 SBS-1000' 이후 기종에서만 기능이 구현됩니다.

내신, 수능, 말하기, 회화
목적은 달라도
시작은 초등코치 천일문!

with
세이펜

• 연계 & 후속 학습에 좋은 초등코치 천일문 시리즈 •

**초등코치 천일문
GRAMMAR 1, 2, 3**
-
1,001개 예문으로
배우는 초등 영문법

**초등코치 천일문
VOCA & STORY 1, 2**
-
1001개의 초등 필수 어휘와
짧은 스토리

쎄듀북닷컴(www.cedubook.com)에서 부가 자료를 무료로 다운로드할 수 있습니다.

쎄듀

1 구문 판매 1위 '천일문' 콘텐츠를 활용하여 정확하고 다양한 구문 학습

끊어읽기　　해석하기　　문장 구조 분석　　해설·해석 제공　　단어 스크램블링　　영작하기

2 문법·서술형 쎄듀의 모든 문법 문항을 활용하여 내신까지 해결하는 정교한 문법 유형 제공

객관식과 주관식의 결합　　문법 포인트별 학습　　보기를 활용한 집합 문항　　내신대비 서술형　　어법+서술형 문제

3 어휘 초·중·고·공무원까지 방대한 어휘량을 제공하며 오프라인 TEST 인쇄도 가능

영단어 카드 학습　　단어 ↔ 뜻 유형　　예문 활용 유형　　단어 매칭 게임

4 선생님 보유 문항 이용

Online Test　　OMR Test

with 세이펜

원어민 음성을 실시간 반복학습	단어 및 대화의 우리말 해석 듣기	선생님의 Workbook Guide로 혼자서도 쉽게 학습

세이펜 핀파일 다운로드 안내

STEP ① 세이펜과 컴퓨터를 USB 케이블로 연결하세요.

STEP ② 쎄듀북 홈페이지(www.cedubook.com)에 접속 후, 학습자료실 메뉴에서 학습할 교재를 찾아 이동합니다.

> 초등교재 ▶ ELT ▶ 학습교재 클릭 ▶ 세이펜 핀파일 자료 클릭
> ▶ 다운로드 (저장을 '다른 이름으로 저장'으로 변경하여 저장소를 USB로 변경) ▶ 완료

STEP ③ 음원 다운로드가 완료되면 세이펜과 컴퓨터의 USB 케이블을 분리하세요.

STEP ④ 세이펜을 분리하면 "시스템을 초기화 중입니다. 잠시만 기다려 주세요." 라는 멘트가 나옵니다.

STEP ⑤ 멘트 종료 후 세이펜을 〈Oh! My Speaking〉 표지에 대보세요.
효과음이 나온 후 바로 학습을 시작할 수 있습니다.

참고사항

◆ 세이펜은 본 교재에 포함되어 있지 않습니다. 별도로 구매하여 이용할 수 있으며, 기존에 보유하신 세이펜이 있다면 핀파일만 다운로드해서
바로 이용하실 수 있습니다.

◆ 세이펜에서 제작된 모든 기종(기존에 보유하고 계신 기종도 호환 가능)으로 사용이 가능합니다.

◆ 모든 기종은 세이펜에서 권장하는 최신 펌웨어 업데이트를 진행해 주시기 바랍니다.
업데이트는 세이펜 홈페이지(www.saypen.com)에서 가능합니다.

◆ 핀파일은 쎄듀북 홈페이지(www.cedubook.com)와 세이펜 홈페이지(www.saypen.com)에서 모두 다운로드 가능합니다.

◆ 세이펜을 이용하지 않는 학습자는 쎄듀북 홈페이지 부가학습자료, 교재 내 QR코드 이미지 등을 활용하여 원어민 음성으로 학습하실 수 있습니다.

◆ 기타 문의사항은 www.cedubook.com / 02-3272-4766으로 연락 바랍니다.

WORKBOOK

Oh! My SPEAKING 1

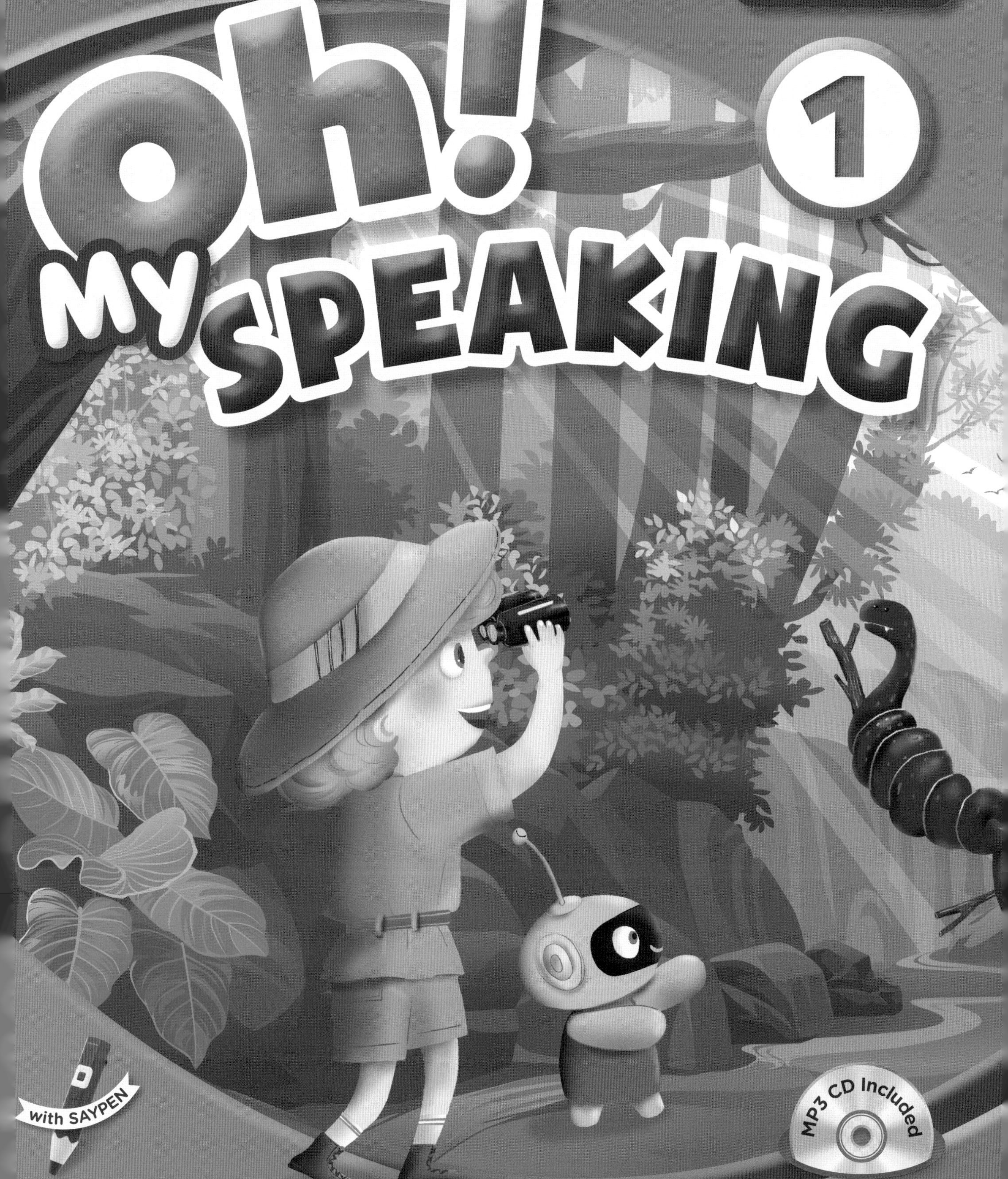

SAYPEN TV www.saypen.com

CEDUBOOK

Oh! My SPEAKING 1

WORKBOOK

CEDU BOOK

UNIT 01 It's a robot.

A Unscramble the words.
(HELP)

1

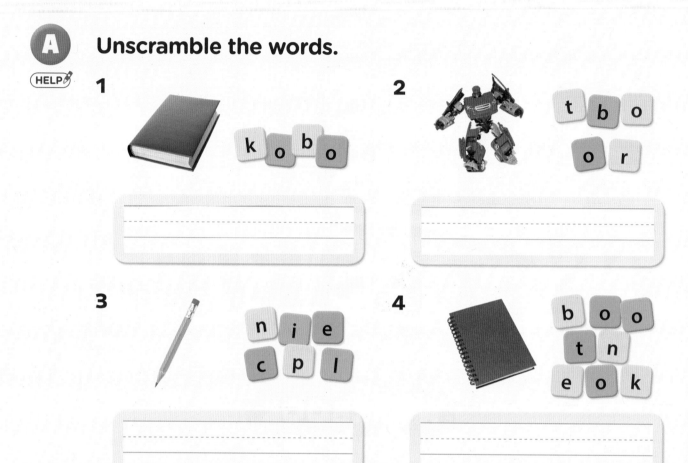

k o b o

2

t b o
o r

3

n i e
c p l

4

b o o
t n
e o k

B Look and write.
(HELP)

1

It's a _____

2

It's not a _____

C Trace and write.

a crayon   a ruler   a chair   a clock   a desk

1

What is it?

It's   .

2

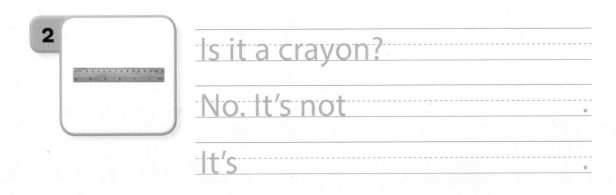

Is it a crayon?

No. It's not   .

It's   .

3

What is it?

It's   .

4

Is it a clock?

Yes. It's   .

D Listen and choose the right picture.

1 a b c

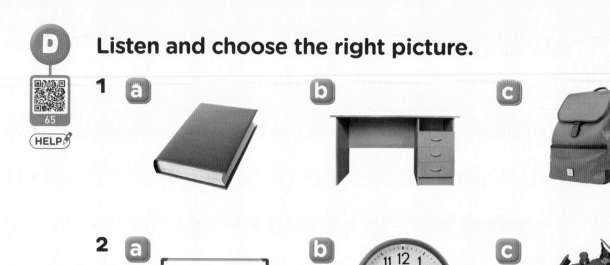

2 a b c

E Listen and choose the right sentence for the blank.

1

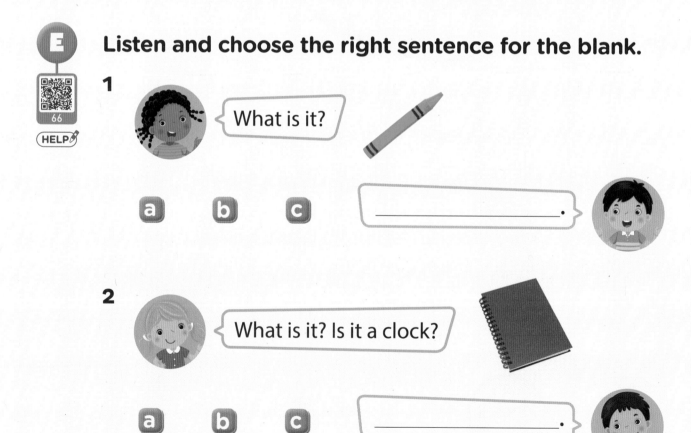

What is it?

a b c

_____ .

2

What is it? Is it a clock?

a b c

_____ .

F Choose the right answer for the blank.

HELP

a It's a robot

b It's a present

c It's not a backpack

YOUR TURN! Choose one item and complete the sentence.

It's _____

A Unscramble the words and match.

1 l a l b _____ • •

2 k e t i _____ • •

3 o l d l _____ • •

4 e z p u z l _____ • •

B Look and write.

1

This is a _____

2

That's a _____

C Trace and write.

| a top | a yo-yo | a jump rope | a toy car |

1

What's this?

This is

2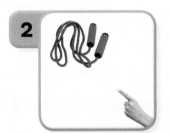

What's that?

That's

3

What's this?

This is

4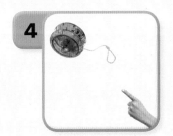

What's that?

That's

D Listen and number.

E Listen and choose the right sentence for the blank.

1

What's this?

_____.

2

What's that?

_____.

Choose the right answer for the blank.

Nice to meet you. I'm Jack.

Nice to meet you, too. I'm Wacky.

What's this?

_____

What's that?

_____.

This is my toy truck, and that's your toy car.

Wow! _____ my toy car. Thank you.

a That's a toy car   **b** This is

c This is a toy truck

YOUR TURN! Choose one item and complete the sentence.

This is a _____.

I'm hungry.

A Complete the puzzle.

(HELP)

DOWN ↓   ACROSS →

1 sad   3 full

2 hungry   4 angry

B How are you feeling? Look and write.

(HELP)

1   I'm _____

2   I'm _____

3   I'm _____

C

Trace and write.

| angry | sleepy | scared | excited | thirsty |

1

Are you _____?

Yes. I'm _____.

2

Are you _____?

Yes. I'm _____.

3

Are you _____?

Yes. I'm _____.

4

Are you angry? _____

No. I'm not _____.

I'm _____.

D Listen and choose the right picture.

1

2

3

4

E Listen and choose the right sentence for the blank.

1

Are you angry?

   _____ .

2

Are you bored?

   _____ .

F Choose the right answer for the blank.

HELP

_____.
Are you hungry, too?

Yes. I'm hungry, too.
Let's go home.

I'm full.
Thank you, Mom.

You're welcome.

_____,
Wacky?

No. I'm not okay.
I'm tired.

Now, are you still tired?

No. _____.
I'm okay! Thank you.

a Are you okay

b I'm not tired

c I'm hungry

YOUR TURN! Look at the pictures and describe the feeling.

I'm _____.

I'm _____.

I'm _____.

UNIT 04 It's a big monster.

A Match and fill in the blanks.

HELP

1   •   •   n __ __

2   •   •   __ o __ __

3   •   •   o __ __

4   •   •   __ __ o r t

B Look and write.

HELP

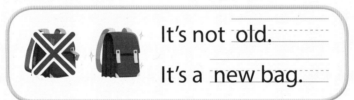

It's not old.

It's a new bag.

1   It's not _____ .

   It's a _____ .

2   It's not _____ .

   It's a _____ .

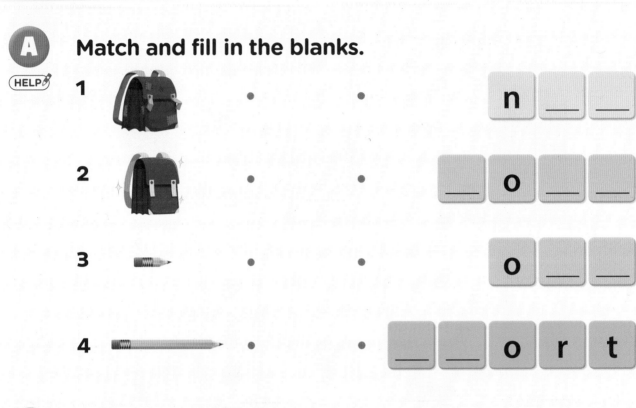

Trace and write.

old	a new backpack	long	a long pencil
thick	a thick book	big	a small ball

1

It's _____

It's _____

2

It's not _____

It's _____

3

It's _____

It's _____

4

It's not _____

It's _____

D Listen and number.

71

(HELP)

E Listen and choose the correct sentence to describe the picture.

72
(HELP)

1

ⓐ   ⓑ   ⓒ

2

ⓐ   ⓑ   ⓒ

Choose the right answer for the blank.

HELP

a It's not a short pencil

b It's not a big monster

c It's big

YOUR TURN! Choose one item and complete the sentences.

It's _____.

It's a/an _____.

UNIT 05 He's my dad.

 HELP

A Unscramble the words.

1 p d a n a g r

_____

2  a n g m a r d

_____

3 c e u n l

_____

4  u s c o n i

_____

B Look and write.

HELP

1

She's my m_____ .

She's kind._____

2

He's my b_____ .

He's friendly._____

C Trace and write.

HELP

1
aunt

Who's she?

She's my

She's cheerful.

2
brother

Who's he?

He's my

He's active.

3
sister

Who's she?

She's my

She's shy.

4
dad

Who's he?

He's my

He's smart.

D Listen and choose the right picture.

73
HELP

1

2

3

4

E Listen and choose the right sentence for the blank.

74
HELP

1 Who's he?

a   b   c

2 Who's she?

a   b   c

F Choose the right answer for the blank.

Who's he?
_____.
He's smart.

Who's she?
_____.
She's kind.

Who's she?
She's my sister.
_____.

Who's he?
How small!
This is my baby brother.

a She's shy

b He's my dad

c She's my grandma

 **YOUR TURN!** Talk about your mom and dad.
Complete the sentences.

smart	kind	friendly	active	cheerful

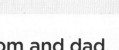

He's my dad. He's _____.

She's my mom. She's _____.

Is it tall?

A Unscramble the words and match.

(HELP)

1   s t f a _____ •   •

2   n s o t r g _____ •   •

3   a t l l _____ •   •

4   s o w l _____ •   •

B Look and write.

(HELP)

| tall | short | strong |

1      Look! A bear!

It's _____

2      Look! A giraffe!

It's not _____

It's _____

C Trace and write.

HELP

| tall | heavy | fast | slow | noisy |

1

Is it _____?

Yes. It's _____.

2

Is it fast?

No. It's not _____.

It's _____.

3

Is it _____?

Yes. It's _____.

4

Is it _____?

Yes. It's _____.

D Listen and number.

E Listen and choose the right sentence for the blank.

1

 Is it fast?

   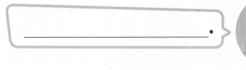

2

 Is it weak?

Choose the right answer for the blank.

HELP

Look! A giraffe!

Is it tall?

Yes. _____.

Wow! A bear!

_____?

Yes! It's big and strong.

Watch out! Is it a snake?

Eek! It's a snake. It's long.

Is it a rock?

No. It's a turtle. _____.

a Is it big

b It's slow

c It's tall

YOUR TURN! Choose one animal and complete the sentences.

Look! A _____! It's _____

UNIT 07 They're dogs.

A Complete the puzzle.

(HELP)

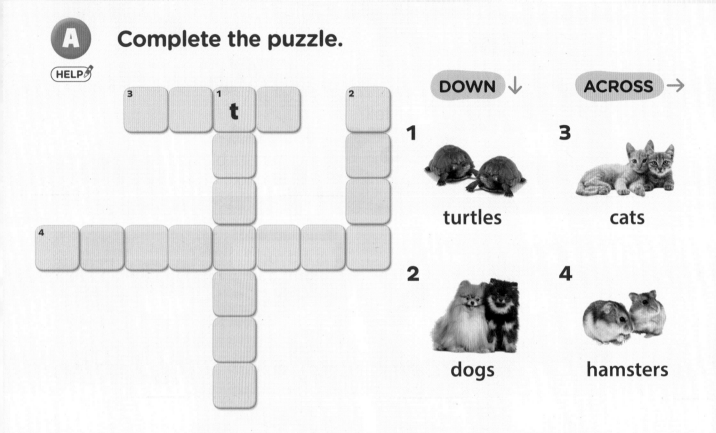

DOWN ↓

ACROSS →

1 turtles

3 cats

2 dogs

4 hamsters

B What are they? Look and write.

(HELP)

1 They're _____

2 They're _____

3 They're _____

C Trace and write.

HELP

| beetles | turtles | chickens | snails | pigs |

1

Are they _____ ?

Yes. They're _____ .

2

Are they _____ ?

Yes. They're _____ .

3

Are they _____ ?

Yes. They're _____ .

4

Are they turtles? _____

No. They're not _____ .

They're _____ .

D Listen and choose the right picture.

1

a **b**

2

a **b**

3

a **b**

4

a **b**

E Listen and choose the right sentence for the blank.

1
 Are they dogs?

a **b** **c**
_____.

2
 Look at them.
Are they parrots?

a **b** **c**
_____.

F Choose the right answer for the blank.

- **a** They're not rabbits
- **b** They're dogs
- **c** They're hamsters

YOUR TURN! Look at the pictures and complete the sentences.

They're

They're

There's a table.

A Match and fill in the blanks.

HELP

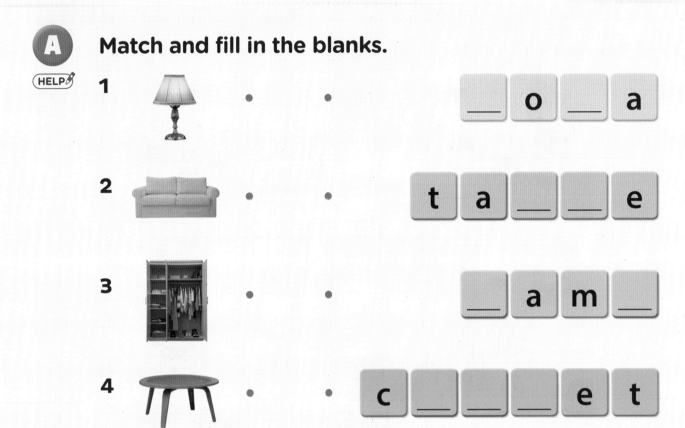

1 ___ o ___ a

2 t a ___ ___ e

3 ___ a m ___

4 c ___ ___ ___ e t

B Look and write.

HELP

1 There's a _____

2 There are _____

C Trace and write.

HELP

curtains	pictures	a rug	a bookshelf

1 What's in the room?

There's

2 What's in the room?

There are

3 What's in the room?

There's

4 What's in the room?

There are

D Listen and number.

E Listen and choose the right sentence for the blank.

1  What's in the room?

 a b c _____.

2 What's in the room?

 a b c _____.

F Choose the right answer for the blank.

HELP

Oh no! My phone!

Wacky, what's in the room? Show me.

Let's see. There's a table.
_____.

_____.
There are books on the sofa.

There's your bag.

There it is.
_____
in the bag.

a There's a sofa

b There are books

c There's your phone

YOUR TURN! Choose one item and complete the sentences.

There's a _____

There are _____

WORKBOOK GUIDE

- Try to do the workbook activities on your own as much as possible.
- If you need additional help or want to hear the answers, scan the appropriate QR code below using your phone.
- You will be able to listen to the teacher's explanation immediately!

UNIT 01

A   B   C   D   E   F

UNIT 02

A   B   C   D   E   F

UNIT 03

A   B   C   D   E   F

UNIT 04

A   B   C   D   E   F

UNIT 05

 A B C D E F

UNIT 06

 A B C D E F

UNIT 07

 A B C D E F

UNIT 08

 A B C D E F

Oh! My Speaking is a six-level speaking series designed for young learners. With task-based activities and vivid illustrations, *Oh! My Speaking* allows students to build up their confidence in speaking and to communicate with their peers in fun and interesting ways. By focusing on basic key words and key patterns with *Oh! My Speaking*, students set out on the journey toward becoming strong speakers of English.

Oh! My Speaking Series

SAYCODE II
S2 SAYPEN
Oh! My Speaking
SD4-OHMS

세이펜과 함께 배우는 Oh! My Speaking

〈Oh! My Speaking〉은 세이펜이 적용된 도서입니다. 세이펜을 가져다 대면 원어민의 생생한 영어 발음과 억양을 듣고 영어 말하기 연습을 할 수 있습니다.

*번역 기능 | 세이펜으로 책을 찍어서 원어민 음성을 들은 후, T 버튼을 짧게 누르면 우리말 해석 음원을 들을 수 있습니다.

✎ 세이펜을 대면 유닛명을 들을 수 있습니다. T 기능 지원

✎ QR코드에 세이펜을 대면 해당 MP3파일이 재생됩니다.

✎ 세이펜을 대면 Activity의 지시문을 들을 수 있습니다. T 기능 지원

✎ 그림이나 영어 단어에 세이펜을 대면 원어민의 발음을 들을 수 있습니다. T 기능 지원

✎ 세이펜을 대면 그림에 해당하는 영어 단어를 들을 수 있습니다. T 기능 지원

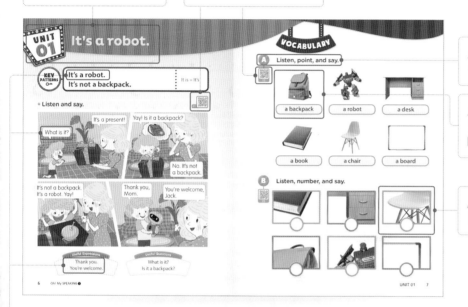

✎ 영어 문장에 세이펜을 대면 원어민의 정확한 발음과 억양을 들을 수 있습니다. T 기능 지원

✎ 번호에 세이펜을 대면 해당 그림에 대한 Key Pattern 대화가 재생되며, 그림이나 영어 단어에 세이펜을 대면 해당하는 영어 단어를 들을 수 있습니다. T 기능 지원

✎ 영어 문장이나 단어에 세이펜을 대면 원어민의 정확한 발음과 억양을 들을 수 있습니다. T 기능 지원

✎ 그림에 세이펜을 대면 해당 그림에 대한 Key Pattern 대화를 들을 수 있습니다. T 기능 지원

✎ 문제 번호에 세이펜을 대면 해당 문제의 음원이 재생되며, 말풍선에 세이펜을 대면 해당 문장 또는 정답 영어 문장을 들을 수 있습니다. T 기능 지원

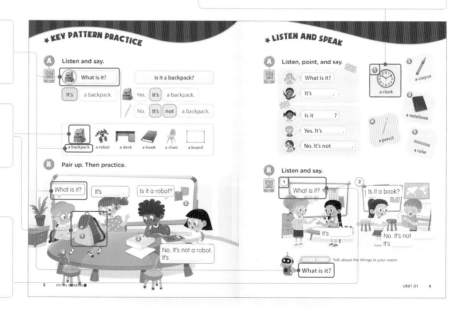

📎 문제 번호에 세이펜을 대면 해당 문제의 음원이 재생됩니다. ⊤기능 지원

📎 문제 번호에 세이펜을 대면 해당 문제의 음원이 재생됩니다.

📎 세이펜을 대면 각 선택지를 들을 수 있습니다. ⊤기능 지원

📎 세이펜을 대면 활동 방법을 들을 수 있습니다. 말풍선에 세이펜을 대면 해당 영어 문장을 들을 수 있습니다. ⊤기능 지원

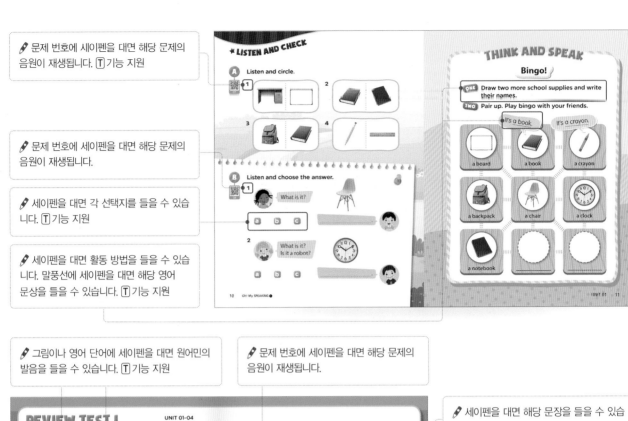

📎 그림이나 영어 단어에 세이펜을 대면 원어민의 발음을 들을 수 있습니다. ⊤기능 지원

📎 문제 번호에 세이펜을 대면 해당 문제의 음원이 재생됩니다.

📎 세이펜을 대면 해당 문장을 들을 수 있습니다. ⊤기능 지원

📎 세이펜을 대면 각 선택지를 들을 수 있습니다. ⊤기능 지원

📎 그림에 세이펜을 대면 해당 문제를 들을 수 있습니다. ⊤기능 지원

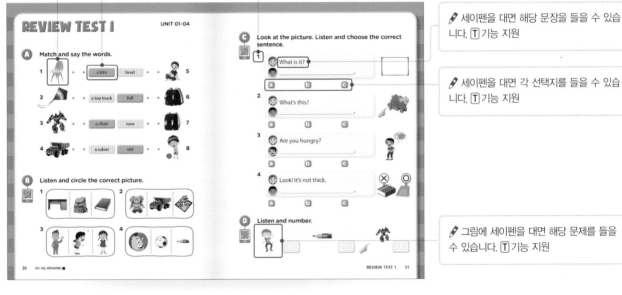

📎 세이펜을 대면 선생님의 Workbook Guide를 들을 수 있습니다. HELP🖊

📎 그림 또는 빈칸에 세이펜을 대면 정답 영어 단어를 들을 수 있습니다. ⊤기능 지원

📎 그림 또는 빈칸에 세이펜을 대면 정답 문장 또는 전체 대화를 들을 수 있습니다. ⊤기능 지원

📎 세이펜을 대면 해당 영어 단어를 들을 수 있습니다. ⊤기능 지원

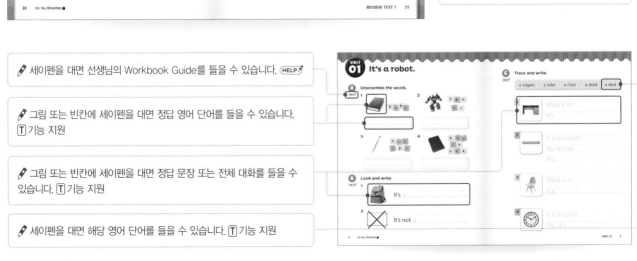